How to Start, Run & Grow a Successful

NONPROFIT ORGANIZATION

DIY Startup Guide to 501 C(3) Nonprofit Charitable Organization For All 50 States & DC

By

Aaron Sanders

Lost River

Publishing House

Cover design

Sam Addison

First Edition

TABLE OF CONTENTS

WHAT IS A NONPROFIT

A nonprofit organization is basically a corporation formed for not-for-profit purposes. The nonprofit legal structure is established at a state level and when the corporation is formed they declare a not-for-profit purpose. Just because you get a 501(c)(3) or other federal tax exemption status doesn't mean your corporation is nonprofit. You can even choose to start a nonprofit organization without applying for federal tax exemption.

You can often easily recognize a nonprofit by their altruistic mission. Some examples of a nonprofit include:

- ☐ A public charity supporting a cause.
- ☐ A private foundation supporting public charities.
- ☐ Churches or religious organizations.
- ☐ Fraternal organizations like homeowners' association.

Just because a corporation is nonprofit doesn't mean it can't produce profits. The difference is that for-profit businesses will distribute profits to shareholders while nonprofit corporations will reinvest their profits into the corporation or the cause it supports. Nonprofit corporations don't pay dividends to investors, but they do pay salaries to employees and invest in building a strong corporation. Let's consider some type of nonprofit organizations.

TYPES OF NONPROFIT ORGANIZATIONS

According to the federal government there are 29 different types of organizations that are tax exempt under the Internal Revenue Code Section 501(c). This can even include businesses like credit unions, civic leagues and chambers of commerce. Before you form your nonprofit you need to make sure you identify your desired 501(c) tax exemption so you can make sure you are using the appropriate language in your articles of incorporation and other necessary documents.

SECTION 501(C)(3)

The most popular section of a nonprofit according to the federal government is 501(c)(3). These are commonly organizations that are called charitable organizations. There are some IRS restrictions that these organizations need to follow.

First, these organizations can't be organized to benefit private interests, such as those related to, directly or indirectly controlled by the private interests.

Second, the organizations need to follow the specific organization and operation guidelines that the IRS identifies in Section 501(c)(3).

Lastly, any of these organizations can't take part in electioneering, campaigning activities or other political activities.

Charitable organizations are further classified by the IRS into public charities or private foundations. The classification is often based on the generation of revenue and activities of the organization.

The IRS defines public charities as follows: "those that (i) are churches, hospitals, qualified medical research organizations affiliated with hospitals, schools, colleges and universities, (ii) have an active program of fundraising and receive contributions from many sources, including the general public, governmental agencies, corporations, private foundations or other public charities, (iii) receive income from the conduct of activities in furtherance of the organization's exempt purposes, or (iv) actively function in a support relationship to one or more existing public charities."

Further the IRS defines private foundations as follows: "typically have a single major source of funding (usually gifts from one family or corporation rather than funding from many sources) and most have as their primary activity the making of grants to other charitable organizations and to individuals, rather than the direct operation of charitable programs."

Other parts of Section 501(c) include other nonprofit organizations. Part 4 include civic leagues or organizations that promote social welfare or focus their net earnings on charitable, educational or recreational purposes. Part 5 includes labor, agricultural or horticultural organizations.

Part 6 includes business leagues, chambers of commerce, real-estate boards, boards of trade or professional football leagues that aren't organized for the purposes of profit. Part 7 includes any club organized for pleasure, recreation or other nonprofit purposes. Part 8 covers fraternal beneficiary societies, orders or associations. Now that we know what a nonprofit is, let's look at why you should consider starting a nonprofit.

WHY START A NON-PROFIT

A nonprofit is a popular structure that has been very successful for public charities. This is because of the many benefits it offers, including the following:

- ☐ Directors enjoy limited liability protection.
- ☐ State and federal tax exemptions.
- ☐ Grant reviewers can evaluate proposals based on the nonprofit corporate model.
- ☐ Donors know and feel comfortable donating to nonprofit corporations.

Let's take a moment to consider the differences between nonprofit and for-profit businesses.

FOR-PROFIT VERSUS NON-PROFIT

Before you start filing any documents, you want to have a clear goal for how your organization is going to be classified in both federal and state records. At one time the distinction between nonprofit and for-profit businesses was clear, but now more and more corporations are finding it better to have a combination of both.

As a result, there are organizations with legal structures such as B-Corporations, L3Cs and Flexible Benefit Corporations. The first decision you need to make is whether your business is going to be nonprofit or for-profit.

The simplest way is to determine if your organization will obtain a 501(c) federal income tax exemption if it won't then don't start a nonprofit. There are five things to ask yourself whether or not your organization can be a nonprofit.

1. Does your organization's primary purpose follow traditional 501(c) exemption?

2. If your organization is going to collect any business income known as unrelated business income, you can lose your 501(c) status if you don't pay taxes on this portion. You should try to determine this before filing.

3. Where will you seek funding? Most nonprofits get their funding from donations, grants, membership

dues and other tax-exempt income sources. For-profits attract investors and can obtain loans.

4. What level of control do you want? For-profit corporations are controlled by shareholders who vote, and a founder can have control with 51% or more of shares. A nonprofit founder will have a community-based leadership from a Board of Directors.

5. As the founder, how are you compensated? A nonprofit still offers you a reasonable salary, but you should still have an exit strategy in mind since you can't simply sell a nonprofit.

As I talked a little about before, there is also the option of creating a for-profit and nonprofit organization that works in tandem. Let's look at some of these legal structures in brief.

MIXED LEGAL STRUCTURES

A newer type of corporation is the B Corporation or Benefit Corporation. This is a for-profit corporation that meets social and environmental performance standards along with rigorous accountability and transparency. This type of organization is best for those that attract large investments and reward investors while also giving directors additional licenses to make decisions for nonprofit goals instead of shareholder profits.

Another option if you live in the state of California is a Flexible Purpose Corporation (FPC). These corporations need to specify at least one "social purpose" in the charter and protect the boards and management from shareholder liability. This type of corporation is typically used for for-profit companies that want traditional investment options.

Another option for for-profit companies is low-profit limited liability companies or L3Cs. The structure of these companies helps bridge the gap between for-profit and nonprofit investing by mirroring federal tax stands for the purpose of program-related investing or PRI. This structure allows a company to preserve the tax flexibility of a traditional LLC.

If a nonprofit is unincorporated or chooses not to incorporate, they are still subject to some legal and taxation requirements. The members of these corporations don't have limited liability protection. This structure is best for those who want to perform short-term community service or fundraising activities.

Before starting a nonprofit, another thing you want to consider is the advantages and disadvantages involved. Let's look at these so you can decide if starting a nonprofit is a good option for you.

ADVANTAGES AND DISADVANTAGES OF STARTING A NON-PROFIT

While starting a nonprofit seems like a worthy cause, it's not without disadvantages. It is easy to become overwhelmed by all the regulations and rules a nonprofit needs to follow. Before you start nonprofit, it can be a good idea to consider both the advantages and disadvantages of a nonprofit corporation to make sure you are ready for what's to come.

THE ADVANTAGES

Nonprofit corporations have the benefit of existing for a long time, potentially even after their founders are gone. As long the purpose of a nonprofit is relevant and continues to generate revenue they can stay in business.

If you have a mission and want to do something to help others, then starting a nonprofit is your best way to organize others around your cause and expand your efforts to have the best possible impact.

Nonprofit corporations protect you from personal liability. This means you and your employees are not personally liable for any debts from the nonprofit. This means if someone chooses to sue your corporation they can only go after the entity and not your personal assets.

Perhaps the best-known advantage is the fact that you don't have to pay taxes so all of your earnings can go back into the cause and further it.

People are more likely to help fund a nonprofit since donations are tax deductible. As long as you have a clear mission and a strategy to gather donations, you will be able to receive adequate funding for your nonprofit.

Another funding option for nonprofits is government grants, many of which are only open to nonprofit corporations.

If a nonprofit is large enough, you can even offer employee benefits. A large nonprofit can still qualify for group discounts on health care or life insurance programs.

THE DISADVANTAGES

The biggest disadvantage with a nonprofit involves the time and cost of starting it. Starting a nonprofit often takes months and can cost close to a thousand dollars just in IRS application fees. Depending on your knowledge you may even need to hire a consultant to help you startup your nonprofit.

In addition, there is the disadvantage of maintaining your nonprofit. You will need to submit annual filings and comply with incorporation laws. There are a lot of activities that can impact your nonprofit status.

The success of your nonprofit depends entirely on volunteers. Your board members are volunteers who can either be experienced professionals or those who don't know much about running an organization. Similarly, employees need the motivation to work for a corporation that isn't paying them and sometimes requires them to work long hours.

Lastly, some nonprofits face funding difficulty. While there are plenty of funding options for nonprofits, it can still be a constant struggle. You have to find funding and compete with the over one million nonprofits in the United States alone.

If you still want to start a nonprofit then let's consider some questions you should ask yourself before getting started.

QUESTIONS TO ASK BEFORE STARTING A NON-PROFIT

As you can tell from the above advantages and disadvantages, starting a nonprofit can be a bit challenging. However, it is doable as the over one million nonprofits in the United States can attest to. If you're still on the fence about whether or not starting a nonprofit is right for you then try asking yourself the following questions:

- ☐ Is there a clear need in your community for a nonprofit with your mission?

- ☐ Do you have a solid financing plan for the organization from the start up to the future?

- ☐ What does it cost to start your nonprofit?

- ☐ Where will you get startup funding and operational funds?

- ☐ How will your nonprofit make an impact on the community?

☐ Is your nonprofit the right solution for your

community?

If you're ready to proceed, let's look at the overview of the startup process, so you have an idea of what's to come.

OVERVIEW OF THE PROCESS

The first step when it comes to starting a nonprofit is to incorporate as a nonprofit corporation in your state. Once you file your articles of incorporation with your state, you will be officially starting your corporation since you are also finalizing the name and establishing an effective day of formation. When you file, it is important that you know what type of 501(c) tax exemption you are going to pursue so you can incorporate it into your documents.

Next, you want to build the foundation of your organization by recruiting and electing a board of directors, appointing officers to the board of directors and creating all key policies and bylaws.

At the same time, you should also be getting tax identification numbers for both your federal and state taxes. You need to apply to the IRS for a Federal Employer Identification Number (FEIN). In some states you are able to apply for a consolidated registration process while in other states you need to apply for unique tax accounts.

The most difficult step in the process of forming a nonprofit organization is to apply for 501(c) federal income tax exemption. You need to know the 501(c) tax exemption you are going for and make sure you are filling out the appropriate form entirely. At the end of this book, you'll find a guide for each individual state to help you through the process based on where your business will be.

Lastly, you need to complete a charitable solicitation registration before you can solicit funds or hire someone to solicit funds. These requirements also vary based on the state where your business will be. This is a key step as it gives you the funds you need to keep your business going.

This is just a quick and simple overview to give you an idea of the process that is involved in starting a nonprofit. We are now going to look at each of these steps in detail and follow it up with a step by step guide for each state.

GETTING STARTED

THE STARTUP CHECKLIST

Before we get started on discussing the process of starting a nonprofit, let's get you a checklist so you can make sure you get everything done.

- ☐ Choose an Appropriate Legal Structure

- ☐ Identify the Desired Federal Tax Exemption Level

- ☐ Recruit Board of Directors According to State Governance Requirements

- ☐ Understand the Incorporation Requirements for Your State

- ☐ Prepare and File the Articles of Incorporation

- ☐ Prepare and Ratify Your Bylaws

- ☐ Obtain an EIN

- ☐ Obtain a State Tax ID

- ☐ Apply for 501(c) Tax Exemption Status

- ☐ Apply for State Tax Exemption Status

☐ Register for Charitable Solicitation in Your State

☐ Obtain an IRS Determination Letter for Tax

Deductible Donations

Now that you have a checklist in place let's start looking at the specifics.

ESTABLISHING BYLAWS

The main governing document of your nonprofit corporation is the nonprofit bylaws. The bylaws help to supplement rules that are already defined by the state corporations' code and help guide how a nonprofit is run.

When you file for federal tax exemption, the IRS asks you to attest to the fact that the bylaws have been adopted or request that you include a copy with your application. The bylaws are used to guide the actions and decision making of your board of directors while helping to prevent or resolve disagreements or conflicts.

You bylaws need to answer important questions such as how you add individuals to the board of directors and how long someone can serve. A nonprofit corporation shouldn't operate without clear bylaws and following applicable state statutes.

You should regularly review the bylaws to make sure they reflect how you operate your corporation. It may be necessary to occasionally amend your bylaws. You should make a note whenever you make revisions and track amendment dates.

Changes should also be reported to the IRS through the annual Form 990. Here is a link to the IRS website where you can view and download the pdf version of this form.

https://www.irs.gov/pub/irs-pdf/f990.pdf

Bylaws need to cover the following topics:
- ☐ Name and Location of the Corporation
- ☐ Purpose of the Nonprofit
- ☐ Election, Roles, and Terms of Directors and Officers
- ☐ Membership
- ☐ Compensation and Indemnification of Directors
- ☐ Amendment of Bylaws
- ☐ Dissolution

DEVELOPING A CONFLICT OF INTEREST POLICY

A conflict of interest policy is important for a nonprofit since it protects the corporation's interest when it enters a transaction or arrangement that might benefit a private interest of key personnel or might result in a possible excess benefit transaction. The conflict of interest policy will supplement applicable state and federal laws for nonprofit corporations.

The board of directors have the primary responsibility of providing oversight to the corporation. Public trust in a nonprofit can be compromised if there are undisclosed conflicts of interest. Having a strong conflict of interest policy that is regularly reviewed and signed annually by the directors and other key personnel can help make sure you protect your corporation as well as the leadership behind it.

A good conflict of interest policy should include the following:

☐ A disclosure statement signed by directors and key personnel annually.

- ☐ A set process for reviewing potential conflicts.
- ☐ A set process for handling any conflicts when they arise.
- ☐ Consequences for violating policy.

As with the bylaws, the IRS will typically ask for you to either attest to or provide a copy of your conflict of interest policy when applying.

ARTICLES OF INCORPORATION

The articles of incorporation for a nonprofit is a legal document that is filed with the secretary of state in order to create the nonprofit corporation. The entire process is called incorporating. Depending on the state you live in, the articles of incorporation can also be referred to as a certificate of incorporation or corporate charter.

There are several benefits you get from choosing to incorporate your nonprofit corporation:

1. You are able to register your corporation's unique trade name.
2. The personal liability of directors and members is limited.

3. The corporation is given additional credibility.
4. It makes it easier to apply for 501(c) federal tax exemption.

Once you have registered your corporation name by filing your articles of incorporation, you can then use that name to apply for a Federal Employer Identification Number or FEIN. It will also allow you to get a business license and sign contracts. You'll need three things before filing your articles of incorporation:

1. The type of nonprofit you want to form.
2. The specific 501(c) tax exemption you want to apply for.
3. The name of the board of directors.

Corporations are often overseen by the secretary of state in most states. State websites will often provide you with templates for articles of incorporation as well as instructions. You can also check the appendix at the end of this book for specifics.

Your articles of incorporation will be approved by the secretary of state as long as they contain the minimum amount of information required by the corporation's code in your state, but there are additional provisions you should include. Again there is a table at the end of this book to help you see what you want to have included.

You don't need someone to help you file articles of incorporation since anyone can act as an incorporator. The state fees to process the articles of incorporation can range from $50 to $400 and can take anywhere from two to four weeks to process.

Some states will offer an expedited filing fee. If your filing is rejected, it can take months more to process, so you want to make sure you have everything right the first time.

There are some states where you are required to publish a notice of intention to file for articles of incorporation. Make sure you check the back of this book for all of the requirements in your state.

LEGAL REQUIREMENTS

LEGAL STRUCTURE OF A NONPROFIT

Before you start a nonprofit, it is important that you have a clear focus on how your organization is going to be classified according to both federal and state records. Know why you are forming a nonprofit organization and what you want to accomplish. The answer to these two questions can help you determine the legal structure of your organization.

When filing for your 501(c) status, you will need to provide a "statement of corporate purpose" in the articles of incorporation. This description needs to complement the narrative of your nonprofit activities accomplished as a part of its mission.

The legal structures of a nonprofit are formed under state law, meaning each state may have slightly different options. There are also several different options for federal tax exemption. Often when starting a nonprofit, the best thing to do is to form your nonprofit at the state level and then apply for 501(c) federal tax exemption status.

This type of legal structure is typically called a charitable organization. The IRS will require specific language in your formation documents that aren't always required in state templates, so it is important to be clear about the direction you want to go before you start.

TAX IDs

Before starting a nonprofit, another important step is to obtain a tax identification or ID number in order to identify yourself to both state and federal taxes. Your tax ID number doesn't change because of your tax exemption, and it won't require separate nonprofit tax ID numbers.

Federally, the IRS requires all new nonprofit organizations to get a Federal Employer Identification Number (FEIN). This is a number your organization will use when paying taxes, opening a bank account or hiring employees. Think of it like a social security number for your organization. You can get a FEIN by filing a Form SS-4 with the IRS.

Depending on the state you live in, you will also be issued one or more tax identification numbers for your organization. Some states automatically give your registration information to the state department of revenue and give you a corporate tax ID(s). Make sure you check for the specific procedures in your state or check out my 50 State Guide to Starting a nonprofit guidebook for your state's particular requirements.

Here is the link to IRS website where you can view and apply for your EIN,

https://www.irs.gov/businesses/small-businesses-self-employed/apply-for-an-employer-identification-number-ein-online

HOW TO BECOME TAX EXEMPT

You tax-exempt status as a nonprofit is obtained from the IRS and from the state where you are going to be operating your nonprofit. The most common tax exemption is 501(c)(3) that gives charitable nonprofits exemption from paying federal corporate income taxes.

States also provide nonprofits with a variety of exemptions from corporate taxes and other imposed taxes such as sales and use taxes. Being exempt from taxes can greatly reduce or completely eliminate the tax burden of your nonprofit corporation. However, just because you are exempt doesn't mean you can avoid filing regular documents with the appropriate authorities.

The Internal Revenue Code 501(c) outlines the options for tax exemption as we've already discussed. The most popular is 501(c)(3) which applies to both public charities and private foundations. Some organizations like churches are automatically exempt from taxes and aren't required to apply for an exemption.

However, these organizations can still seek IRS recognition in order to assure their contributors that their donations are tax deductible. A corporation needs to file for federal exemption within 27 months of their formation date. The IRS will issue a determination letter that details whether or not an exemption is granted and whether or not donors can make tax-deductible contributions.

State tax exemptions can vary, so you need to take a look at the table at the end of this book that shows you the income and sales tax exemptions for each state. You should seek an exemption for each state in which your nonprofit operates. Depending on your state you may be exempt from income, sales, use and other taxes faced by nonprofits.

Often exemption requires you to submit an application to the department of revenue in your state with a renewal every one to five years.

Here is the page on IRS website where you can find out up-to-date information on their requirements.

https://www.irs.gov/charities-non-profits/charitable-organizations/exemption-requirements-section-501c3-organizations

GETTING AN IRS DETERMINATION LETTER

Getting an IRS determination letter notifies you that your application for federal tax exemption status under Section 501(c)(3) is approved. This is a great day for you as you start your nonprofit. There are several unique advantages you get by having an IRS determination letter:

☐ You are exempt from paying federal taxes.

☐ Donors to your nonprofit can claim their contributions on their annual tax returns.

- You can get discounts on USPS postage rates and other goods and services.

- You can apply for grant funding that is often restricted only to tax-exempt corporations.

- Your mission gains additional credibility.

Once you have your IRS determination letter there are a few additional things you want to do:

- Exempting your corporation from sales and other state taxes.

- Register to fundraise for your corporation in the 41 states that require registration before you can ask for donations and make sure you have appropriate disclosure statements.

- Be aware of ongoing requirements like filing the IRS Form 990 in order to maintain your federal exemption status.

☐ Store and keep your determination letter in a records kit and keep an electronic copy on hand as well.

BUILDING THE STAFF

NONPROFIT GOVERNANCE

The governance of your nonprofit is another term for how you administer your nonprofit. There are several key players in a nonprofit organization, including the following:

- ☐ Directors

- ☐ Officers

- ☐ Committees

- ☐ Members

- ☐ Executive Director

- ☐ Staff

- ☐ Volunteers

Each of these positions plays a key role in completing the mission of your nonprofit corporation.

Under the law, all corporations are a legal entity. The corporation is distinct and separate from those who run it.

The corporation can be a part of contracts, be sued and perform other powers that are allowed under state law. All of these activities are carried out through the actions of a board of directors or designee.

At the end of this book, you'll find a chart showing the governance requirements for each state. Let's look at each position.

BOARD OF DIRECTORS/TRUSTEES

These are the strategic leaders of the nonprofit corporation, and they follow the mission statement of the corporation. These individuals are responsible for establishing goals and making decisions.

Individual directors have limited power while decisions are made as a board group. A minimum number of directors known as a quorum needed to vote in order to take action. Once the board makes a decision, it is documented through resolutions, which are then transmitted into the actions of the corporation.

We'll discuss a little bit more about the board of directors soon.

OFFICERS OF THE BOARD

These individuals are elected by the board of directors and often include the following:

- [ ] President/Chair to preside over board meetings.
- [ ] Secretary to record meeting minutes.
- [ ] A treasurer who oversees finances.
- [ ] One or more Vice Presidents/Vice Chairs.

COMMITTEES

These can also be established by the board of directors. If a corporation has a large board of directors, it can be good to delegate areas like research, oversight, and authority to committees.

Committees can be responsible for such things as recruiting new board members, conducting orientation and evaluating the performance of board members and directors. Committees can be made up of both directors and non-directors.

MEMBERS

This isn't a requirement of a corporation's governance structure. In fact, most public charities don't have members. In mutual benefit corporations or other such corporations that have members, they have rights such as voting to elect directors.

Membership may have multiple classes, qualifications, and dues. Members can have additional administrative oversight and can be important for corporations that want to engage and represent the interests of individuals and communities.

CEO AND EXECUTIVE DIRECTOR

These positions are typically given to a single member of the board of directors. The primary responsibility of this individual is to carry out the direction of the board of directors.

Staff and volunteers report to the CEO/Executive Director. This individual is a conduit for communication between the board and the team that runs the corporation. The board of directors oversee the performance and compensation of this individual.

STAFF AND VOLUNTEERS

These people make up the front lines of your nonprofit corporation. This includes W-2 employees, independent contractors, and unpaid volunteers. Their director comes from the CEO/Executive Director, and they report directly to them.

FRIENDS GROUP/ADVISORY BOARD

Sometimes these are referred to as "members," but they don't have voting rights or legal provisions that come with true membership. This is why they are termed different, so their distinction is clear. They are helpful in providing an informal opinion and perspective while staying separate from the formal workings of a nonprofit corporation.

BOARD OF DIRECTIONS

Most states require a nonprofit to have an initial board of director before filing articles of incorporation and require a minimum number of directors as long as the corporation is in business.

The statutory corporation's code for the state where you're incorporated will define the requirements and responsibilities of the board of directors. Other rules are defined by corporate bylaws. Make sure your review the nonprofit code for your state to completely understand all rules that apply to your board of directors.

The following are some general rules for the board of directors:

☐ The board of directors sets the mission and goals for the corporation.

☐ The directors themselves have limited power, as a board, they vote and present decisions.

☐ Members of the board are not compensated and work as volunteers.

☐ Directors elect officers to the board.

☐ Directors have limited liability and are protected from debts and legal actions against the nonprofit corporation.

There are three main legal duties that the board of directors need to meet in addition to their other responsibilities:

1. Each director is required to demonstrate a duty of care by attending, staying informed and making decisions that are in the best interest of the corporation and its mission.

2. Directors cannot achieve personal gain through their role and need to protect confidentiality while disclosing and avoiding potential conflicts of interest.

3. Directors must carry out their duties in obedience by following the nonprofit mission and corporate purpose. This includes complying with internal corporate and external government regulations.

CLASSIFYING EMPLOYEES

One of the most common mistakes that a nonprofit corporation makes is misclassifying workers. Making this mistake can lead to IRS penalties as well as violations of state and federal wage and hour laws.

This is why it is important to make sure your workers are properly classified as employees and independent contractors and as exempt or non-exempt employees.

WHY IT'S IMPORTANT

If you misclassify workers, then you will end up owing penalties, back taxes, and back pay. The first thing you need to know is the difference between an independent contractor and an employee. If a person is an employee, then you need to know if they are "exempt" or "non-exempt" from overtime.

Classifying correctly is based on two layers of definitions: state and federal. Twenty-eight states follow federal Fair Labor Standards Act or FLSA while others have different rules that apply. Let's talk a little more about appropriate classification.

AN EMPLOYEE OR INDEPENDENT CONTRACTOR

One common issue is when a nonprofit classifies a worker as an independent contractor when that person is actually an employee under federal DOL or state wage and hour laws. If you violate this, you will be responsible for unpaid wages including overtime as well as state/federal withholding taxes and all associated penalties. The following are some points to consider:

☐ Employees have position descriptions while independent contractors don't.

☐ Independent contractors sign a written contract describing the scope of work and show that the independent contractor is responsible for their own income taxes and insurance coverage.

☐ Check the IRS as well as state law definitions to distinguish employees from independent contractors in your state.

NON-EXEMPT OR EXEMPT

Another area where classification becomes an issue is when a nonprofit wrongly considers an employee to be exempt from overtime payments when a federal or state labor law classifies the work as non-exempt. This can result in you owing the worker compensation for overtime and potential penalties. Keep the following points in mind:

- ☐ Even if a worker is "salaried," they can still be entitled to overtime hours beyond 40 hours in a workweek based on federal rules. But there are always exceptions to this rule. For example, if you have a salaried employee who often works 70 hours each week instead of 40, the labor board can check to determine if they are getting paid enough (or above the minimum wage) by dividing their total hours by the salary amount. If this number falls below the minimum wage, then you can get into a lot of trouble.
- ☐ States vary in their wage and hour rules that determine which workers are entitled to overtime and what makes workers exempt. You should check your state for specific wage and hour guidelines/regulations.

- ☐ It can be a good idea to institute a policy requiring workers to get advanced authorization from a supervisor before working overtime.

- ☐ When you prepare any budget documents, make sure you anticipate any potential overtime.

RECRUITING VOLUNTEERS

Every nonprofit needs volunteers to operate efficiently. However, the difficult part is finding the right volunteers and convincing them to help your effort. There are many ways that you can recruit volunteers, but the key is finding the appropriate methods for your corporation and its needs.

Let's look at three basic ways you can recruit volunteers for your nonprofit.

INFORMATION/BROAD RECRUITMENT

If you need to get a large number of volunteers together in a short period of time and you don't have any qualified tasks that need to be performed, then you should consider this method of recruitment. With this method you need to focus on disseminating as much information as possible through the following methods:

- ☐ Brochures

- ☐ Posters

- ☐ Public Speaking

- ☐ Media Notices

- ☐ Word of Mouth

TARGETED RECRUITMENT

This is the method of recruitment you use when you need to attract a specific type of volunteer. With this, you are looking for people with specific skills rather than broad characteristics. For this type of recruitment you need to answer the following questions:

- ☐ What does your corporation need?

- ☐ Who is able to provide what your corporation need?

- ☐ What is the best way to reach these people?

- ☐ What would motivate these people to volunteer for your corporation?

Working through these questions helps you to find the ideal volunteers for your corporation. Once you find your volunteers you simply need to take your recruitment methods directly to the source.

CONCENTRIC CIRCLES RECRUITMENT

This type of recruitment focuses on individuals who are already directly or indirectly linked to your corporation and then get your recruiting message to them. This means recruiting people that are familiar with your corporation and the cause you address. These individuals can be the easiest to convince to volunteer than others.

RECRUITMENT MESSAGE

No matter which of the methods you choose to use for recruiting, you need to have a strong message. Make a person understand why your corporation is worth their time. A recruitment message needs to be short, simple and direct. While you want to stress the need for their service in the community you should also be able to point out benefits the individual will receive.

PAYING EMPLOYEES

Most nonprofit corporations operate with volunteers who simply provide voluntary, uncompensated services. However, there are also nonprofit corporations who hire employees that have compensation and working conditions based on the federal and state laws.

When you choose to hire an employee you are faced with a number of legal requirements; from filing with the state to determining adequate wages/compensation and calculating withholdings for tax purposes.

HOW MUCH SHOULD YOU PAY?

Even tax-exempt charitable nonprofits are required to pay minimum wage. A requirement of maintaining tax-exempt status is providing compensation that is reasonable and not excessive.

When hiring a new staff member, you should know what the going rate is by comparing salary and benefits information from other nonprofits in your area with a similar mission.

Employees must be paid the legal minimum wage that varies by state or by the federal minimum wage. Employees should be paid whichever is higher. If employees work over 40 hours a week, a nonprofit may still owe these employees for overtime.

FUNDRAISING

FUNDRAISING COMPLIANCE

If you are going to raise funds from the public, then you need to comply with charitable solicitation registration requirements. The state is responsible for charitable solicitation regulation, and the requirements vary by state.

Forty-one states require nonprofits to register in order to solicit residents, and twenty-five states require specific information to be disclosed on solicitation materials. In this last chapter of the book, we will look at the steps you need to take to maintain compliance for fundraising.

WHY IT'S IMPORTANT

For starters, charitable solicitation registration requirements are law and shouldn't be taken lightly. In addition, donors prefer corporations that are transparent about their fundraising activities. In fact, there is a rise in charity rating websites. A corporation that registers for charitable solicitation becomes a trustworthy company.

While the requirements are difficult, it provides corporations with a chance to show how serious they are to their donors.

In addition, many grant applications and other funding sources can only be filed once the charitable registration is completed. It is easy to see while getting charitable registration is beneficial.

UNLICENSED SOLICITATION

The penalties for unlicensed solicitation varies by state and can be quite severe. If you solicit donations prior to registering, if you file late renewals or if you face complaints from the public you may be faced with the following penalties:

- ☐ State fines, late fees and penalties.
- ☐ Civil and criminal action against directors and officers.
- ☐ Revocation of tax exemption.
- ☐ Denial of rights to solicit donations.
- ☐ Negative public views.

- ☐ Damaged relationships with grant makers and donors.

- ☐ Loss of grants and/or donations.

REGISTRATION REQUIREMENTS

First, you need to understand just what charitable solicitation is. To put it simply, charitable solicitation is the act of asking for something valuable. This can involve many forms including fundraising events, direct solicitation, and online fundraising.

Then this brings you to the definition of charitable registration or fundraising registration. This is a process where a nonprofit corporation becomes licensed to ask for funds in a specific state.

It is a process that involves filing paperwork to the state charities bureau which is often overseen by the state attorney general or secretary of state.

These registrations are in place to protect donors from illegitimate corporations that solicit funds for non-charitable causes.

APPLICATIONS

Applying for charitable registration typically involves submitting a specific form based on your state, a filing fee and supporting documentation. Applications typically require an IRS Determination Letter, IRS Form 990 and a list of directors and officers among other documents that vary by state.

The fee will also vary by state and is often based on the total gross revenue in the previous year or the contributions received in the state.

EXEMPTIONS

A state can permit for certain entities to avoid filing charitable registration. A corporation that qualifies for exemptions often needs to submit an exemption request or other paperwork in place of a traditional application. Exemptions are often based on corporation specific factors. Often a determining factor is the solicitation methods a corporation uses.

Even if the exemption is awarded, a corporation will still need to keep track of changing jurisdiction requirements, prepare necessary applications, manage renewals and monitor any changes in annual contributions.

RENEWAL REQUIREMENTS

As with the initial application, renewals need to be submitted at regular intervals in order to keep the charities bureau up to date on changes in a registrant's status and financials. Due dates vary by states but typically is based on the number of months since the close of a corporation's fiscal year.

ESTABLISHING CHARITABLE SOLICITATION DISCLOSURES

At least twenty-five states require you to have some type of disclosure statement when you communicate with donors. These disclosures need to be included with written solicitations, donor confirmations, donor receipts and contribution reminders. However, specifics will vary by state.

The basic goal of the disclosure is to convey where a person can obtain information about the nonprofit. Disclosure statements are also used by donors to make informed decisions about who they donate to.

Before you think about putting a donate button on your website as a simple way to get money for your nonprofit take the time to consider what is involved in online fundraising. Online fundraising requires unique regulatory challenges for a nonprofit corporation.

NATIONWIDE REGISTRATION

Online fundraising is generally considered nationwide since it can reach people in all states. Most states don't have specific laws for soliciting online, but rather consider these under the category "other media." The requirements vary by state and also the laws, forms and procedures are always changing.

This means that charities need to register in all jurisdictions where soliciting is done. To make this process easier, corporations need to file for nationwide registration.

TARGETED REGISTRATION

However, not all corporations have the resources needed to register in every state that has requirements. This means a more measured approach is best. Perhaps one of the easiest solutions is to clearly state on your website which jurisdictions you can accept donations from.

FIVE ONLINE DONATION TIPS

1. Always make sure you register in the state where you incorporate.

2. Following up with a donor that contributes through your website will trigger registration requirements in the state where they are located.

3. Soliciting through a charity portal backed by donor-advised funds doesn't trigger registration.

4. Online solicitation occurs at any time you provide people with a way to contribute to your corporation. This means that even if you use a third-party site or an offline donation method, it will still trigger registration requirements.

5. Social media can be used to send out information about your corporation, and you won't need to register. However, if your language mentions solicitation in any form, then you will need to register. Unless the promotion of donations comes from a fan independent of your corporation.

PROFESSIONAL FUNDRAISING

Another option for a nonprofit is to hire a professional to fundraise or solicit donations. Before hiring a professional, you still need to comply with charitable solicitation registration laws.

Professional fundraisers or solicitors are companies or individuals that provide fundraising services. Professional fundraisers need to comply with charitable solicitation registration laws in forty-five states.

Professionals who help ask for funds for nonprofits are very heavily regulated and scrutinized. Professionals who help charities, but don't interact with the public don't have as much oversight.

Individual solicitors face requirements in fifteen jurisdictions:

1. Alabama

2. Arkansas

3. Florida

4. Georgia

5. Illinois

6. Kansas

7. Kentucky

8. Michigan

9. Mississippi

10. Missouri

11. New Jersey

12. New York

13. Oklahoma

14. Rhode Island

15. South Carolina

In these jurisdictions, individual solicitors are registered under the same regulatory body as fundraising firms. However, the requirements are less than they would be for firms. These registrations are often renewed on an annual basis.

For a firm that offers professional fundraising services, they need to get licensed before starting charitable solicitation. Firms without a license face penalty fees and possibly even criminal charges. Firms often need to register with the secretary of state. Registration is often divided based on the type of fundraising services a firm provides.

The first is professional solicitors who take an active role in fundraising campaigns and solicit for donations on behalf of the nonprofit that hires them. Since they are directly involved in the solicitation, they face greater regulations.

A second service is fundraising counsel. This is when a firm manages or consults on charitable campaigns, but doesn't actively solicit on behalf of the nonprofit corporation.

Even if you hire a professional, the primary burden for meeting solicitation requirements falls to the nonprofit corporation. The nonprofit needs to meet the following requirements:

- ☐ You should register before engaging in any solicitation efforts.

- ☐ Place a disclosure on charitable solicitation registration forms that you are hiring a professional.

- ☐ Place all required disclosures on solicitation materials.

- ☐ Maintain charitable solicitation registrations by filing appropriate annual renewals and financial reports.

Professional fundraisers are required to comply with registration, reporting and disclosure requirements under the law. This is why it is important you check your professional's compliance before hiring them.

The professional you hire should be compliant with registration, bonding, and recordkeeping requirements.

Make sure you also document your contract in writing with the professional fundraiser.

CO-VENTURES AND CAUSE MARKETING

A commercial co-venturer is when a nonprofit enters into a "share of revenue" contract with a for-profit company. In the for-profit sector, this is known as cause marketing. This type of partnership can benefit both ventures. However, specific licensing is required.

WHO ARE CO-VENTURERS

Many for-profit companies that have a well-developed corporate social responsibility program are choosing to partner with charities. These partnerships have two purposes: a for-profit brand is able to align itself with customer interests while the charity gets the financial benefits of the business.

However, when the private and public sector becomes entwined the government needs to make sure both are kept in check. This means these agreements need to be licensed and both companies and charities need to meet specific obligations.

A charity needs to have solicitation registration to start, and the business needs to get licensed as a commercial co-venturer. 24 states have some form of requirements specific to commercial co-ventures, and most of the filing requirements are the responsibility of the business. Only four states require a formal license, and others require filing a contract, disclosing in advertising, the state-specific language in the contract, some type of accounting or recordkeeping and/or final financial reporting.

A commercial co-venturer is a good thing for charities, but only if you make sure, all the proper licenses are in place.

As with hiring a professional fundraiser, you should independently comply with registration before entering with a commercial co-venture. Most for-profit companies aren't aware of the registration requirements for fundraising, so the charity needs to make sure everything is on the up and up before entering a contract.

CHARITABLE GAMING

A fun way to connect with the community through your charity is with games of chance; it is also a great way to raise funds for your cause. However, there are a lot of state and local government requirements for holding a gaming event.

Most states allow a charity to conduct a range of gaming events as long as they have the proper license. Some of the permitted gaming options include the following:

- ☐ Bingo
- ☐ Raffles
- ☐ Pull-tab Tickets
- ☐ Poker Tournaments
- ☐ Casino Game Nights

Before hosting any of the above events, you need to apply for the relevant license or permit issued by both the state and municipal gaming authorities. Depending on where you plan to hold the event you may need a state level license, a municipal permit or both. If you plan to do more than one type of gaming you may need to apply for more than one license.

States often offer limited exemptions when it comes to charitable gaming laws. For example, a senior living facility offering bingo for social purposes is often exempt. The only states that don't allow charitable organizations to host gaming events in Utah and Hawaii. However, charity raffles are allowed in Hawaii as long as there is no separate fee to enter the raffle.

GAMING LICENSES AND PERMITS

Before applying for the necessary permit or license, you need to make sure you meet the requirements. The requirements will vary by state, but most require a charity to have an IRS tax exemption and an active registration with the secretary of state. Also, most states will only allow applications from corporations that have been in existence a specific number of years.

An application typically includes filing an application and fee with the appropriate regulatory body in your state. Sometimes you'll also need to complete this process at the local level. The following information is often required:

- ☐ Articles of Incorporation

- ☐ Bylaws

- ☐ List of individuals assisting with gaming

- ☐ Location of gaming

- ☐ List of corporate officers

Most states also require a nonprofit to designate a specific individual to oversee gaming activities.

HOSTING A GAMING EVENT

Once you have a license, it is important you understand what the license allows you to do. Some licenses are only good for a single event, while others last longer. There are also often restrictions on the length of the event as well.

During the gaming event, you also need to follow all applicable rules. Most states don't allow minors to be involved in gaming activities and have limits on the total value of prizes awarded. You will also need to track receipts that come in from the event for reporting purposes.

RENEWING A GAMING LICENSE

Charitable gaming licenses are good for variable periods of time. Single-use permits that are only good for a single event cannot be renewed. However, most nonprofits can apply for multiple permits throughout the year.

Other charitable gaming licenses are issued for a calendar year and allow a nonprofit to hold multiple gaming events throughout the year. Most do have the restrictions that you can only hold one event per week for 52 weeks. These licenses have expiration dates and can be renewed for additional periods.

NONCOMPLIANCE

If you host a gaming event without the proper licenses, it can be costly. Penalty fees will vary by state, but some may be higher than the amount you raise at the event. For example, in New Jersey, the penalty can be up to $7,500 for violating bingo and raffle laws. This is why it is important to follow charitable gaming laws.

CHARITABLE GIFT ANNUITY

Charitable gift annuities are a benefit for both the nonprofit corporation as well as the donor. With a charitable annuity contract, a donor provides a lump-sum donation in exchange for tax benefits and a stream of income that lasts for the life of the donor.

After the performance of the contract, charities will receive all remaining funds. This is a powerful tool that allows charities to get sizeable donations and gives donors a chance to support a charity of their choice.

Since these agreements have a complex financial nature, states tend to have significant regulations on them. Regulations and requirements are often based on the location of the donor, the regulations involved and the requirements that can apply. If you plan to use charitable gift annuities as a way to fund your nonprofit, then pay careful attention.

GIFT ANNUITY REQUIREMENTS

Nearly all states allow charities to use gift annuities as a fundraising option. This method of fundraising is typically regulated by the department of insurance, and if your donors are in more than one state, you will need to register in multiple states. Some common requirements include the following:

- ☐ 501(c)(3) status
- ☐ Disclosure statements on annuity contracts
- ☐ Age requirements for corporations
- ☐ Financial asset requirements
- ☐ Audited financial statements
- ☐ Creating a separate reserve account
- ☐ Submitting sample annuity agreements

States requirements can be grouped into four separate categories as follows:

STATES REQUIRING REGISTRATION

This is found in fourteen states:

1. Alabama
2. Arkansas
3. California

4. Florida

5. Hawaii

6. Maryland

7. Montana

8. New Hampshire

9. New Jersey

10. New York

11. North Dakota

12. Oklahoma

13. Tennessee

14. Washington

In these states, you need a license or registration before you can issue charitable gift annuities. The requirements will vary by state, but most require the submission of an application along with the necessary fees and additional information.

STATES THAT REQUIRE NOTIFICATION

This is required in the following states:

1. Alaska

2. Connecticut

3. Georgia

4. Idaho

5. Iowa

6. Mississippi

7. Missouri

8. Nevada

9. New Mexico

10. North Carolina

11. Texas

12. West Virginia

These states require a nonprofit to submit a statement acknowledging a desire to issue gift annuities. The time frame can range from the first day to as late as 90 days from the issuance of the first annuity.

STATES THAT DO NOT REQUIRE NOTIFICATION

This is followed in the states:

1. Arizona

2. Colorado

3. Illinois

4. Indiana

5. Kansas

6. Kentucky

7. Louisiana

8. Maine

9. Massachusetts

10. Minnesota

11. Nebraska

12. Oregon

13. Pennsylvania

14. South Carolina

15. South Dakota

16. Utah

17. Vermont

18. Virginia

19. Wisconsin

In these nineteen states, you don't need to register or notify the department of insurance before issuing a gift annuity. However, you still need to meet prerequisites before issuing the annuity and need to follow regulations throughout the fundraising process.

STATES WITH NO STATUTORY PROVISIONS

Six states have no statutes that specifically address charitable gift annuities:

1. Delaware

2. District of Columbia

3. Michigan

4. Ohio

5. Rhode Island

6. Wyoming

In these states, charities are allowed to issue annuities, but you may need to meet prerequisites. You should seek additional guidance before issuing an annuity in these states.

ONGOING COMPLIANCE

Once you meet the requirements for filing initially, charities need to follow guidelines continuously that are set by the state. This typically includes submitting annual renewal filings, but some states don't require ongoing filings.

CONCLUSION

As you can see, there isn't that much involved in starting a nonprofit. It is more about doing it right the first time. In addition to the general process outlined in this book, check out the following appendixes to help you quickly find the requirements for your individual states.

Take a look at the state by state guide to help you complete the startup process.

Last but not the least, I want to say THANK YOU for purchasing and reading this book. I really hope you got a lot out of it! Despite our best efforts, if you found any errors or typos in my work, please forgive me as this was my first try at writing such guides, I promise I will get better.

Can I ask you for a quick favor though?

If you enjoyed this book, I would really appreciate it if you could leave me a Review.

I LOVE getting feedback from my wonderful readers, and reviews really do make the difference. I read all of my reviews and would love to hear your thoughts.

Thank you and god bless.

APPENDIX-1

LIST OF FILING REQUIREMENTS BY STATE

ALABAMA

1. Name Reservation Request Form
2. Name Reservation Certificate
3. Form SOSDF-5
4. Bylaws
5. IRS Form SS-4
6. IRS Form 1023
7. IRS Determination Letter
8. Form COM-101
9. Charitable Organizations Registration Statement or Charitable Organizations Registration Exemption

Cost	Time
Name Reservation: $28	24 hours
Incorporation: $100 state + $50 county	4 days to about 6 weeks
501(c): $275 or $600	2 weeks to 3 months
Charitable Registration: $25	

ALASKA

1. Form 08-438: Articles of Incorporation
2. Initial Report
3. Form 08-4181: Business License Application
4. Bylaws
5. IRS Form SS-4
6. IRS Form 1023
7. IRS Determination Letter
8. Charitable Organizations Annual Registration Form

Cost	Time
Incorporation: $50	About 10-15 days by mail. Immediate online.
Business License: $50	About 10-15 days by mail. Immediate online.
501(c): $275 or $600	2 weeks to 3 months
Charitable Registration: $40	

ARIZONA

1. Form CFCVLR: Cover Sheet
2. Form CF0041: Articles of Incorporation
3. Form C082: Director Attachment

4. Form C084: Incorporator Attachment

5. Form M002: Statutory Agent Acceptance

6. Form CF0001: Certificate of Disclosure

7. Bylaws

8. IRS Form SS-4

9. IRS Form 1023

10. IRS Determination Letter

11. Form JT-1: State Tax Registration

12. URS Charitable Registration

Cost	Time
Incorporation: $40 Expedite: $35	About two months. About 7-10 days.
Publishing of Incorporation: About $200	
State Taxes: $12 per license/location	
501(c): $275 or $600	2 weeks to 3 months

ARKANSAS

1. Form NPD-01: Articles of Incorporation

2. Bylaws

3. IRS Form SS-4

4. IRS Form 1023

5. IRS Determination Letter

6. Form AR-1R: Combined Business Tax Registration Form
7. Form AR1023CT: Application for Income Tax Exempt Status
8. Form F0003: Streamlined Sales and Use Tax Agreement Certificate of Exemption
9. URS Charitable Registration
10. Charitable Organization Application for Registration or Verification of Exemption from Registration

Cost	Time
Incorporation: $45-50	About 2-4 days
501(c): $275 or $600	2 weeks to 3 months

CALIFORNIA

1. Articles of Incorporation:
    a. Form ARTS-MU - Mutual Benefit Corporation
    b. Form ARTS-PB - Public Benefit Corporation
    c. Form ARTS-RE - Religious Corporation
    d. Form ARTS-CID - CID Corporation
2. Form SI-100: Statement of Information

3. Bylaws
4. IRS Form SS-4
5. IRS Form 1023
6. IRS Determination Letter
7. Form FTB-3500: Exemption Application or Form FTB-3500a: Submission of Exemption Request
8. URS Charitable Registration

Cost	Time
Incorporation: $30/mail, $45/person	
Optional Preclearance Service: $250-500	
Optional Expedite: $350-500	
Statement of Information: $20	About 1 days
501(c): $275 or $600	2 weeks to 3 months
FTB Exemption: $25	
Charitable Registration: $25	

COLORADO

1. Form ARTINC_NPC: Articles of Incorporation
2. Bylaws

3. IRS Form SS-4

4. IRS Form 1023

5. IRS Determination Letter

6. Form CR-0100: Sales Tax Withholding Account Application

7. Form UITL-100: Application for Unemployment Insurance Account and Determination of Employer Liability

8. Form DR-0715: Application for Sales Tax Exemption

9. Form DR-0716: Statement of Non-Profit

10. Charitable Registration

Cost	Time
Incorporation: $50	Immediate
501(c): $275 or $600	2 weeks to 3 months
Charitable License: $8	
Charitable Registration: $10	

CONNECTICUT

1. Form CIN-1-1.0: Certificate of Incorporation

2. Form COS-1-1.0: Organization and First Report

3. Bylaws

4. IRS Form SS-4

5. IRS Form 1023

6. IRS Determination Letter

7. Form REG-1: Business Tax Registration

8. CERT-119: Purchases of Tangible Personal Property and Services

9. Initial Charitable Organization Registration Application

Cost	Time
Incorporation: $50 Expedite: $50	About 3-5 days. About 24 hours.
First Report: $50	
501(c): $275 or $600	2 weeks to 3 months
Charitable Registration: $50	

DELAWARE

1. Certificate of Incorporation Cover Letter

2. Form INCNSTK09: Certificate of Incorporation or Form INC-Exempt

3. Bylaws

4. IRS Form SS-4

5. IRS Form 1023

6. IRS Determination Letter

7. Form CRA: Combined Registration Application

8. Form UC-1: Report to Determine Liability

9. URS Charitable Registration

Cost	Time
Incorporation: $89 + $9 for extra pages	About 3 weeks
Optional Expedite Fee: $50-1000	$50=24 hours, $100=Same Day, $500=2 hours, $1000=1 hour
Delaware Form CRA: Varies	
501(c): $275 or $600	2 weeks to 3 months

DISTRICT OF COLUMBIA

1. Form DNP-1: Articles of Incorporation

2. Bylaws

3. IRS Form SS-4

4. IRS Form 1023

5. IRS Determination Letter

6. Form FR 500: Tax Registration

7. Form FR 164: Tax Exemption

8. URS Charitable Registration

9. Basic Business License for the Charitable Solicitation Category or General Business License

10. Charitable Gaming License

Cost	Time
Incorporation: $80 Expedite: $50-100	About 15 days. $50=About 3 days. $100=Same day.
501(c): $275 or $600	2 weeks to 3 months
Business License: $412.50 or $324.50	Immediate to 3 weeks
Charitable Gaming License: $10-500	Immediate to 3 weeks

FLORIDA

1. Form CR2E006: Nonprofit Articles of Incorporation

2. Bylaws

3. IRS Form SS-4

4. IRS Form 1023

5. IRS Determination Letter

6. Form DR-1: Business Tax Application

7. Form DR-5: Application for Consumer's Certificate of Exemption

8. URS Charitable Registration
9. Form FDACS-10100: Solicitation of Contributions Registration Application or Form FDACS-10110: Exempt Charitable Organizations/Sponsors Application.

Cost	Time
Incorporation: $70	About 1-3 days online. About 8-17 days mail.
501(c): $275 or $600	2 weeks to 3 months
Sales Tax License: $5	
Charitable Registration: $10-400	

GEORGIA

1. Articles of Incorporation
2. Data Transmittal Form 227
3. Notice of Incorporation
4. Initial "Annual" Registration
5. Bylaws
6. IRS Form SS-4
7. IRS Form 1023
8. IRS Determination Letter

9. Form 3605: Application for Recognition of Exemption

10. URS Charitable Registration

11. Form C-100: Charitable Organization Registration

Cost	Time
Incorporation: $100	About 5-12 days.
Notice of Incorporation: $40	
Initial "Annual" Registration: $50	
501(c): $275 or $600	2 weeks to 3 months
Charitable Registration: $35	

HAWAII

1. Form DNP-1: Articles of Incorporation

2. Bylaws

3. IRS Form SS-4

4. IRS Form 1023

5. IRS Determination Letter

6. Form BB-1: Basic Business Application

7. Form G-6: Application for Exemption from General Excise Tax

8. URS Charitable Registration

9. Charitable Organization Registration or Exemption Application

Cost	Time
Incorporation: $26 Expedite: $25	About 7-14 days by mail. About 3-5 days by fax, person or online. Expedite about 1-3 days.
501(c): $275 or $600	2 weeks to 3 months
Form BB-1: $20	

IDAHO

1. Form 201: Articles of Incorporation

2. Bylaws

3. IRS Form SS-4

4. IRS Form 1023

5. IRS Determination Letter

6. State Tax Registration

7. URS Charitable Registration

Cost	Time
Incorporation: $30 Expedite: $20	About 1 week. About

	1 day.
501(c): $275 or $600	2 weeks to 3 months.

ILLINOIS

1. Form NFP 102.10: Articles of Incorporation
2. Bylaws
3. IRS Form SS-4
4. IRS Form 1023
5. IRS Determination Letter
6. Form REG-1: Business Registration Application
7. Sales Tax Exemption Letter of Request
8. URS Charitable Registration
9. Form CO-1: Charitable Registration Statement

Cost	Time
Incorporation: $50/mail. $77.75/online	About 2 weeks. About 1-5 days.
Expedite: $100	About 1-5 days.
501(c): $275 or $600	2 weeks to 3 months
Form REG-1: varies	
Charitable Registration: $15	

1. Form 4162: Articles of Incorporation
2. Bylaws
3. IRS Form SS-4
4. IRS Form 1023
5. IRS Determination Letter
6. Form BT-1: Business Tax Application
7. Form NP-20A: Nonprofit Application for Sales Tax Exemption
8. URS Charitable Registration
9. Form CG-QA: Charitable Gaming Qualification Application

Cost	Time
Incorporation: $30	About 15 minutes online. About 24 hours in person. About 5-7 days by mail.
501(c): $275 or $600	2 weeks to 3 months
Form BT-1: $25	
Gaming Qualification	120 days

IOWA

1. Articles of Incorporation

2. Bylaws

3. IRS Form SS-4

4. IRS Form 1023

5. IRS Determination Letter

6. Form 78-005a: Business Tax Registration

7. URS Charitable Registration

Cost	Time
Incorporation: $20	About 1-2 days.
501(c): $275 or $600	2 weeks to 3 months
Business Tax Registration: Varies	

KANSAS

1. Form CN: Articles of Incorporation

2. Bylaws

3. IRS Form SS-4

4. IRS Form 1023

5. IRS Determination Letter

6. Form CR-16: Business Tax Application

7. Sales Tax Exemption Certificate

8. URS Charitable Registration

Cost	Time
Incorporation: $20. Expedite: $20	About 4 days by paper. Immediate online. About 1 day by paper, expedite.
501(c): $275 or $600	2 weeks to 3 months
Business Tax Registration: Varies	
Charitable Registration: $35	

KENTUCKY

1. Form NAI: Articles of Incorporation
2. Bylaws
3. IRS Form SS-4
4. IRS Form 1023
5. IRS Determination Letter
6. Form 10A100: Tax Registration Application
7. Form 51A125: Application for Purchase Exemption - Sales and Use Tax
8. URS Charitable Registration
9. Charitable Registration

Cost	Time
Incorporation: $8	About 3-5 days by mail or online. Immediate in person.
501(c): $275 or $600	2 weeks to 3 months

LOUISIANA

1. Form 395: Articles of Incorporation
2. Initial Report with Recorder of Mortgages
3. Bylaws
4. IRS Form SS-4
5. IRS Form 1023
6. IRS Determination Letter
7. Form R-16019: Application for Revenue Account Number
8. Form R-1048: Application for Exemption from Collection of Sales Tax at Certain Fundraising Activities
9. URS Charitable Registration
10. Charitable Registration

Cost	Time
Incorporation: $75. Expedite: $30-50.	About 1 week. About 24 hours to immediate.
501(c): $275 or $600	2 weeks to 3 months
Charitable Registration: $25	

MAINE

1. Form MNPCA-6: Articles of Incorporation

2. Bylaws
3. IRS Form SS-4
4. IRS Form 1023
5. IRS Determination Letter
6. Application for Tax Registration
7. Sales Tax Exempt Organization Application
8. URS Charitable Registration
9. Charitable Organization Application

Cost	Time
Incorporation: $40. Expedite: $50-100.	About 14 days. About 24 hours or immediate.
501(c): $275 or $600	2 weeks to 3 months
Charitable Registration: $50	

MARYLAND

1. Articles of Incorporation
2. Bylaws
3. IRS Form SS-4
4. IRS Form 1023
5. IRS Determination Letter
6. Form CRS: Combined Registration Application
7. Income Tax Exemption Application
8. Property Tax Exemption Application
9. URS Charitable Registration
10. Form COR-92: Charity Registration

Cost	Time
Incorporation: $100 filing fee	About 10+ weeks.
$20 Organization and Capitalization Fee	
$50 Development Center Fee	
Optional $5 return mail fee	
Optional $50 expedite fee	About 7 days online/fax. The same day in person.
501(c): $275 or $600	2 weeks to 3 months
Charitable Registration: $0-300	

MASSACHUSETTS

1. Articles of Incorporation
2. Bylaws
3. IRS Form SS-4
4. IRS Form 1023
5. IRS Determination Letter
6. Form TA-1: Application for Registration
7. Corporate Excise Tax Exemption Application
8. Property Tax Exemption Application
9. URS Charitable Registration
10. Form PC or Short Form PC: Charitable Registration

Cost	Time

Incorporation: $35	About 2-3 days
501(c): $275 or $600	2 weeks to 3 months
Charitable Registration: $150	6-8 weeks

MICHIGAN

1. Form CSCL/CD-502: Articles of Incorporation
2. Bylaws
3. IRS Form SS-4
4. IRS Form 1023
5. IRS Determination Letter
6. Form 518: Registration for Business Taxes
7. Form 3372: Sales and Use Tax Certificate of Exemption
8. URS Charitable Registration
9. Initial Solicitation Registration Form

Cost	Time
Incorporation: $20. Expedite: $50-1,000	About 5-7 days. Expedite: $50=About 24 hours. $100=Same day. $500=2 hours. $1,000=1 hour.
501(c): $275 or $600	2 weeks to 3 months

MINNESOTA

1. Articles of Incorporation

2. Bylaws
3. IRS Form SS-4
4. IRS Form 1023
5. IRS Determination Letter
6. Form ABR: Revenue Application for Business Registration
7. Form ST16: Revenue Application for Sales and Use Tax Exempt Status
8. Charitable Organization Initial Registration and Annual Report Form

Cost	Time
Incorporation: $70/mail $90/online or in person	About 5-7 days by mail or About 24 hours
501(c): $275 or $600	2 weeks to 3 months
Charitable Registration: $25	

MISSISSIPPI

1. Form F0001: Articles of Incorporation
2. Bylaws
3. IRS Form SS-4
4. IRS 1023
5. IRS Determination Letter
6. Taxpayer Access Point Registration
7. URS Charitable Registration
8. Charitable Organization Registration or Charitable Notice of Exemption

Cost	Time
Incorporation: $50	About 2-3 days.
501(c): $275 or $600	2 weeks to 3 months
Charitable Registration or Exemption: $50	

MISSOURI

1. Form Corp-52: Articles of Incorporation
2. Bylaws
3. IRS Form SS-4
4. IRS Form 1023
5. IRS Determination Letter
6. Online Business Registration or Form 2643: Tax Registration Application
7. URS Charitable Registration
8. Charitable Organization - Initial Registration Statement

Cost	Time
Incorporation: $25	About 1-7 days
501(c): $275 or $600	2 weeks to 3 months
Charitable Registration: $15	

MONTANA

1. Form 54: Articles of Incorporation
2. Bylaws
3. IRS Form SS-4
4. IRS Form 1023
5. IRS Determination Letter
6. Tax Registration
7. Tax Exempt Status Request Form
8. URS Charitable Registration

Cost	Time
Incorporation: $20	About 10 days
501(c): $275 or $600	2 weeks to 3 months

NEBRASKA

1. Articles of Incorporation
2. Bylaws
3. IRS Form SS-4
4. IRS Form 1023
5. IRS Determination Letter
6. Form 20: Tax Application
7. Form 4: Exemption Application for Sales and Use Tax
8. URS Charitable Registration

Cost	Time

Incorporation: $10 + $5/page	About 1-2 days online
Tax Application: $0	
501(c): $275 or $600	2 weeks to 3 months

NEVADA

1. Articles of Incorporation
2. Certificate of Acceptance of Appointment by Registered Agent
3. Initial/Annual List of Officers and Directors
4. State Business License Application or Exemption
5. Charitable Solicitation Registration
6. Bylaws
7. IRS Form SS-4
8. IRS Form 1023
9. IRS Determination Letter
10. Form APP-01.00: Common Business Registration
11. Form APP-02.01: Application for Sales/Use Tax Exemption
12. URS Charitable Registration
13. Nonprofit Corporation Registration Information

Cost	Time
Incorporation: $50. Expedite: $125-1,000	Immediate online
Initial List: $50	
501(c): $275 or $600	2 weeks to 3 months

Business License: $200	

NEW HAMPSHIRE

1. Form NP-1: Articles of Agreement of a New Hampshire Nonprofit Corporation
2. Bylaws
3. IRS Form SS-4
4. IRS Form 1023
5. IRS Determination Letter
6. URS Charitable Registration
7. Form NHCT-1: Application for Registration

Cost	Time
Incorporation: $30	About 10-14 days
501(c): $275 or $600	2 weeks to 3 months
Charitable Registration: $25	

NEW JERSEY

1. Public Records Filing for New Business Entity
2. Bylaws
3. IRS Form SS-4
4. IRS Form 1023
5. IRS Determination Letter
6. Form NJ-REG: Business Registration Form
7. Form REG-1E: Sales Tax Exemption Application
8. URS Charitable Registration

9. Charitable Registration

Cost	Time
Incorporation: $75	About 4 weeks
501(c): $275 or $600	2 weeks to 3 months
Charitable Registration: $30-250	

NEW MEXICO

1. Form DNP: Articles of Incorporation
2. Domestic Nonprofit Corporation Initial Report
3. Bylaws
4. IRS Form SS-4
5. IRS Form 1023
6. IRS Determination Letter
7. Form ACD-31015: Application for Business Tax Identification Number
8. Form ACD-31050: Application for Nontaxable Transaction Certificates
9. URS Charitable Registration
10. NM-COROS Charitable Registration

Cost	Time
Incorporation: $25. Expedite: $100-150	About 3 months. About 1-2 days.
Initial Report: $10	

501(c): $275 or $600	2 weeks to 3 months

NEW YORK

1. New York Agency Approval of Purpose
2. Form DOS1511-f-l: Not-for-Profit Certificate of Incorporation
3. Bylaws
4. IRS Form SS-4
5. IRS Form 1023
6. IRS Determination Letter
7. Tax Registration State and City
8. Form CT-247: Application for Exemption from Corporation Franchise Taxes
9. Form ST-119.2: Application for an Exempt Organization Certificate
10. Property Tax Exemption State and City
11. Form CHAR 410: Registration Statement for Charitable Organizations

Cost	Time
Incorporation: $75. Expedite: $25-150	About 14 days. 24 hours to 2 hours.
501(c): $275 or $600	2 weeks to 3 months.
Charitable Registration: $25	

NORTH CAROLINA

1. Form N-01: Articles of Incorporation
2. Form N-14: Tax-Exempt Status Information
3. Bylaws
4. IRS Form SS-4
5. IRS Form 1023
6. IRS Determination Letter
7. Form NC-BR: Business Registration Application for Income Tax Withholding, Sales and Use Tax, and Machinery and Equipment Tax
8. Form CD-345: Corporate Franchise and Income Tax Questionnaire for Nonprofits
9. Solicitation License Application

Cost	Time
Incorporation: $60. Expedite: $100-200	About 5-7 days. 24 hour to Same Day
501(c): $275 or $600	2 weeks to 3 months
Charitable Registration: $0-200	

NORTH DAKOTA

1. Form SFN-13003: Articles of Incorporation
2. Bylaws
3. IRS Form SS-4
4. IRS Form 1023
5. IRS Determination Letter

6. Form ACD-31015: Application for Business Tax Identification Number
7. Form ACD-31050: Application for Nontaxable Transaction Certificates
8. URS Charitable Registration
9. Form SFN-11300: Charitable Organization Registration Statement

Cost	Time
Incorporation: $40	About 30 days
501(c): $275 or $600	2 weeks to 3 months
Charitable Registration: $25	

Ohio

1. Form 532B: Articles of Incorporation
2. Bylaws
3. IRS Form SS-4
4. IRS Form 1023
5. IRS Determination Letter
6. Business Gateway Tax Registration
7. Form STEC-B: Sales and Use Tax Blanket Exemption Certificate
8. URS Charitable Registration
9. Charitable Organization Registration

Cost	Time

Incorporation: $99	About 3-7 days
501(c): $275 or $600	2 weeks to 3 months
Charitable Registration: $50-200	

OKLAHOMA

1. Form SOS 0009-07/12: Certificate of Incorporation
2. Bylaws
3. IRS Form SS-4
4. IRS Form 1023
5. IRS Determination Letter
6. Form 40001: Business Registration Application
7. Form 13-16-A: Application for Sales Tax Exemption
8. URS Charitable Registration
9. Form SOS 101A-01/13: Registration Statement or Charitable Organization

Cost	Time
Incorporation: $25	About 7-10 days by mail. About 1 day online.
501(c): $275 or $600	2 weeks to 3 months
Business Registration: Varies	
Charitable Registration: $15-65	

OREGON

1. Form 30: Articles of Incorporation
2. Bylaws
3. IRS Form SS-4
4. IRS Form 1023
5. IRS Determination Letter
6. URS Charitable Registration
7. Form RF-C: Registration for Charitable Organizations

Cost	Time
Incorporation: $50	About 7-10 days by mail. About 1-2 days by fax. Immediate online.
501(c): $275 or $600	2 weeks to 3 months

PENNSYLVANIA

1. Form DSCB: 15-5306/7102B-2: Articles of Incorporation
2. Pennsylvania Docketing Statement
3. Pennsylvania Incorporation Publishing
4. Bylaws
5. IRS Form SS-4
6. IRS Form 1023
7. IRS Determination Letter
8. Form PA-100: Enterprise Registration Form
9. Form REV-72: Sales Tax Exemption Application
10. URS Charitable Registration

11. Form BCO-10: Charitable Organization Registration Statement

Cost	Time
Incorporation: $125	About 14 days
Incorporation Publishing: $200	
501(c): $275 or $600	2 weeks to 3 months
PA-100: $0 + fees	Varies
Charitable Registration: $0	

RHODE ISLAND

1. Form 200: Articles of Incorporation
2. Bylaws
3. IRS Form SS-4
4. IRS Form 1023
5. IRS Determination Letter
6. Form BAR: Business Application and Registration
7. Application for Certificate of Exemption for an Exempt Organization from the Rhode Island Sales and Use Tax
8. URS Charitable Registration
9. Charitable Trust Registration Statement

Cost	Time

Incorporation: $35	About 7 days by mail or online. Same day for in person.
501(c): $275 or $600	2 weeks to 3 months
Form BAR: Varies	
Sales Tax Exemption: $25	
Charitable Trust Registration: $50	

SOUTH CAROLINA

1. Form NP: Articles of Incorporation
2. Articles of Incorporation 501(c)(3) Attachment
3. Bylaws
4. IRS Form SS-4
5. IRS Form 1023
6. IRS Determination Letter
7. Form SCDOR-111: Tax Registration Application
8. Form ST-387: Application for Sales Tax Exemption for Exempt Organizations
9. URS Charitable Registration
10. Registration Statement for a Charitable Organization or Application for Registration Exemption

Cost	Time
Incorporation: $25	About 7-10 days by mail. About 1-2 days online.
501(c): $275 or $600	2 weeks to 3 months

Form SCDOR-111: Varies	
Charitable Registration: $50	

SOUTH DAKOTA

1. Articles of Incorporation
2. Bylaws
3. IRS Form SS-4
4. IRS Form 1023
5. IRS Determination Letter
6. Tax License Application
7. Form SD EForm-1932-V10: Streamlined Sales Tax Agreement Certificate of Exemption
8. URS Charitable Registration

Cost	Time
Incorporation: $30 Expedite: $50	About 3-5 days.
501(c): $275 or $600	2 weeks to 3 months.
Tax License Application: Varies	

TENNESSEE

1. Form SS-441B: Charter Nonprofit Corporation
2. Bylaws
3. IRS Form SS-4
4. IRS Form 1023
5. IRS Determination Letter

6. Form RV-F1300501: Application for Registration
7. Form RV-1306901: Application for Registration - Sales and Use Tax Exempt Entities
8. URS Charitable Registration
9. Charitable Registration - Form SS-6001: Application for Registration of a Charitable Organization and Form SS-6002: Summary of Financial Activities of a Charitable Organization OR Form SS-6042: Exemption Request

Cost	Time
Incorporation: $100	About 4 days by mail. About 2 days online. Immediate in person.
501(c): $275 or $600	2 weeks to 3 months
Charitable Registration: $50	

TEXAS

1. Form 202: Certificate of Formation - Nonprofit Corporation
2. Bylaws
3. IRS Form SS-4
4. IRS Form 1023
5. IRS Determination Letter
6. Texas Tax Forms
7. Texas Application for Exemption - Charitable Organizations
8. URS Charitable Registration

Cost	Time
Incorporation: $25	About 3-5 days by mail or fax.
501(c): $275 or $600	2 weeks to 3 months

UTAH

1. Form SS-4418: Charter Nonprofit Corporation
2. Bylaws
3. IRS Form SS-4
4. IRS Form 1023
5. IRS Determination Letter
6. Form TC-69: State Business and Tax Registration
7. Business License Registration
8. Form TC-160: Application for Sales Tax Exemption Number for Religious or Charitable Institutions
9. URS Charitable Registration
10. Charitable Organization Permit Application Form or Request for Exemption pursuant to Charitable Solicitations Act

Cost	Time
Incorporation: $30	About 14 days by mail or fax. About 1 day online.
501(c): $275 or $600	2 weeks to 3 months
Charitable Registration: $100	

VERMONT

1. Articles of Incorporation Form
2. Bylaws
3. IRS Form SS-4
4. IRS Form 1023
5. IRS Determination Letter
6. Form S-1: Application for Business Tax Account
7. Form S-3: Sales Tax Exemption Certificate for Resale and Exempt Organizations
8. URS Charitable Registration

Cost	Time
Incorporation: $125	About 5-7 days
501(c): $275 or $600	2 weeks to 3 months

VIRGINIA

1. Form SCC819: Articles of Incorporation
2. Bylaws
3. IRS Form SS-4
4. IRS Form 1023
5. IRS Determination Letter
6. Form R-1: Business Registration Form
7. Form NPO: Retail Sales and Use Tax Exemption Application
8. URS Charitable Registration

9. Form 102: Charitable Organization Registration or Form 100: Exemption Application for a Charitable or Civic Organization

Cost	Time
Incorporation: $75	About 7 days by mail. About 3-7 days online.
501(c): $275 or $600	2 weeks to 3 months
Charitable Registration: $100 + $30-325 depending on contributions	

WASHINGTON

1. Articles of Incorporation
2. Bylaws
3. IRS Form SS-4
4. IRS Form 1023
5. IRS Determination Letter
6. Form BLS-700-028: Business License Application
7. URS Charitable Registration
8. Charitable Organization Registration

Cost	Time
Incorporation: $30/mail $50/online	About 2 months. About 2-3 days.
Expedited: $80	About 2-3 days

501(c): $275 or $600	2 weeks to 3 months
Business License Application: $19	
Charitable Organization Application: $60	

WEST VIRGINIA

1. Form CD-1NP: Articles of Incorporation with Non-Profit IRS Attachment
2. Bylaws
3. IRS Form SS-4
4. IRS Form 1023
5. IRS Determination Letter
6. Form WV/BUS-APP: Business Registration
7. Form F0003: Certificate of Exemption
8. URS Charitable Registration
9. Form CHR-1: Registration Statement of Charitable Organizations

Cost	Time
Incorporation: $25	About 1-2 days
501(c): $275 or $600	2 weeks to 3 months
Charitable Registration: $15-50	

1. Form 102: Articles of Incorporation
2. Bylaws
3. IRS Form SS-4
4. IRS Form 1023
5. IRS Determination Letter
6. Form BTR-101: Application for Business Tax Registration
7. Form S-103: Application for Wisconsin Sales and Use Tax Certificate of Exempt Status
8. URS Charitable Registration
9. Form 296: Charitable Organization Registration Statement

Cost	Time
Incorporation: $35	About 4-7 days
501(c): $275 or $600	2 weeks to 3 months
Business Tax Registration: $20	
Charitable Registration: $15	

WYOMING

1. Form NP-Articles of Incorporation
2. Bylaws
3. IRS Form SS-4

4. IRS Form 1023
5. IRS Determination Letter
6. Wyoming SSUTA Certificate of Exemption Application
7. URS Charitable Registration

Cost	Time
Incorporation: $25	About 3-5 days
501(c): $275 or $600	2 weeks to 3 months

APPENDIX -2

LIST OF REQUIRED GOVERNANCE BY STATE

ALABAMA

Directors:

- Minimum of 3
- Qualifications:
  - Natural person
  - No residency requirement
  - No membership requirement
- Quorum: Majority
- Committee: Minimum 2 Directors

Officers:

- A president, one or more vice-presidents, a secretary, a treasurer and other officers and assistant officers a necessary.
- Term: 1-year default, 3-year maximum
- Two or more offices can be held by the same individual, expect the positions of president and secretary

Members:

- Optional
- Required annual meeting
- Quorum: 1/10th votes

ALASKA

Directors:

- Minimum of 3
- Qualifications: None
- Term: 1 year
- Quorum: Majority
- Committee: Minimum of 2 directors of the executive committee

Officers:

- A president, one or more vice presidents as outlined in bylaws, a secretary, and a treasurer are required.
- The same individual can hold two or more offices except for the president and secretary.

Members:

- Optional

- Required annual meeting
- Quorum: 1/10th Votes

ARIZONA

Directors:

- Minimum of 1
- Qualifications:
  - An individual
  - No residency requirement
  - No membership requirement
- Term: 1 year
- Quorum: Majority
- Committee: Minimum 1 director

Officers:

- As defined by the bylaws or articles of incorporation. One officer prepares minutes of the directors' and members' meeting and authenticates record of the corporation.
- The same individual may hold two or more offices.

Members:

- Optional

- Required annual meeting
- Quorum: 1/10th Votes

ARKANSAS

Directors:

- Minimum of 3
- Qualifications:
  - An individual
  - No residency requirement
  - No membership requirement
- Term: 1-year default, six-year maximum
- Quorum: Majority
- Committee: Minimum 2 directors

Officers:

- A president, a vice president, a secretary, a treasurer and other officers that are appointed by the board.
- The same individual may hold two or more offices.
- Term: 3 years maximum

Members:

- Optional

- Required annual meeting
- Quorum: 1/10th Votes

CALIFORNIA

Directors:

- Minimum of 1
- Qualifications: None
- Term: 1 year
- Quorum: Majority
- Committee: 2 Directors Minimum
- No directory can vote by proxy

Officers:

- A corporation needs to have a chair of the board or a president or both, a secretary, a treasurer or a chief financial officer or both, and any other officers with titles and duties as laid out in the bylaws.
- Elected by the board.
- The same individual may hold two or more offices except the president cannot serve as the secretary or treasurer.

Members:

- Optional
- Meetings are required in each year when directors are to be elected.
- Quorum: 1/3rd Votes.

COLORADO

Directors:

- Minimum of 1
- Qualifications:
    - An individual
    - No residency requirement
    - No membership requirement
- Term: 1 year
- Quorum: Majority
- Committee: 1 Director minimum

Officers:

- A president, secretary, treasurer and other officers as designed by the board of directors.
- Qualifications: 18 years or older.
- The same individual may hold two or more offices.

Members:

- Optional
- Required annual meetings.
- Quorum: 1/4th Votes.

CONNECTICUT

Directors:

- Minimum of 3.
- Qualifications: None
- Term: Until the next annual meeting.
- Quorum: Majority
- Committee: 1 Director minimum

Officers:

- As defined in bylaws or the articles of incorporation. One officer prepares minutes of the directors' and members' meetings and authenticates the records of the corporation.
- The same individual may hold two or more offices.

Members:

- Optional
- Annual meeting required if members are entitled to vote for the directors.

- Quorum: Majority of entitled voters.

DISTRICT OF COLUMBIA

Directors:

- Minimum of 3
- Qualifications:
    - An individual
    - No residency requirement
    - No membership requirement
- Term: 1-year default, five year maximum
- Quorum: Majority
- Committee: 1 Director minimum

Officers:

- Two separate officers minimum: one to manage the corporation and another to manage the financial affairs. One officer prepares minutes of the directors' and members' meetings and keeps records.
- The same individual may hold two or more offices.

Members:

- Optional

- Required annual meeting
- Quorum: Majority of entitled votes

DELAWARE

Directors:

- Minimum of 1
- Qualifications:
  - Natural person
  - No residency requirement
  - No membership requirement
- Term: Until a successor is elected and qualified
- Quorum: Majority

Officers:

- As defined in the board resolution or bylaws. One officer prepares minutes of the directors' and members' meetings and keeps a record.
- Term: Until a successor is elected and qualified.

Members:

- Required
- Annual meetings required if members are entitled to vote for directors.

- Quorum: 1/3rd Votes

FLORIDA

Directors:

- Minimum of 3
- Qualifications:
  - A natural person age 18 or older
  - One director may be 15 or older if permitted by the bylaws or board of directors
  - No residency requirement
  - No membership requirement
- Term: 1 year
- Quorum: Majority
- Committee: 2 Director minimum

Officers:

- As defined by the bylaws or articles of incorporation. One officer prepares minutes from the directors' and members' meetings and authenticates records.
- Elected by the board of directors
- Term: 1 year
- The same individual can hold two or more offices

Members:

- Optional
- The regular meeting is required as defined in the bylaws or articles of incorporation.
- Quorum: A defined in bylaws or articles of incorporation.

GEORGIA

Directors:

- Minimum of 1
- Qualifications:
    - A natural person over the age of 18
    - No residency requirement
    - No membership requirement
- Term: 1 year
- Quorum: Majority

Officers:

- As defined by the bylaws or articles of incorporation.
- One officer prepares minutes for the directors' and members' meetings and authenticates records.
- The same individual may hold two or more offices.

Members:

- Optional
- Required annual meeting
- Quorum: 1/10th Votes

HAWAII

Directors:

- Minimum of 3
- Qualifications:
    - An individual
    - No residency requirement
    - No membership requirement
- Term: 1-year default, maximum five years
- Quorum: Majority
- Committee: 2 Directors minimum

Officers:

- As defined by the bylaws or articles of incorporation. One officer prepares minutes for the directors' and members' meetings and authenticates records.
- One individual may hold two or more offices.

Members:

- Optional
- Required annual meeting
- Quorum: 1/10th Votes

IDAHO

Directors:

- Minimum of 3. Minimum of 1 for a religious organization.
- Qualifications:
  - An individual
  - No residency requirement
  - Must be a member of a cooperative corporation
- Term: 1-year default, five year maximum
- Quorum: Majority
- Committee: 2 Directors minimum

Officers:

- A president, secretary, treasurer and other officers as appointed by the board.

- An individual may hold two or more offices except that of the president and secretary or in a religious organization.

Members:

- Optional, but required for a cooperative corporation.
- Required annual meeting
- Quorum: 1/10th Votes

ILLINOIS

Directors:

- Minimum of 3
- Qualifications: None
- Term: Until the next election
- Quorum: Majority
- Committee: 2 Director minimum and directors must be the membership majority, except for the committees for electing directors.

Officers:

- As defined in the bylaws or articles of incorporation. One officer certifies the corporate records.
- The same individual may hold two or more offices if provided in the bylaws.

Members:

- Optional
- Required annual meeting
- Quorum: 1/10th Votes

INDIANA

Directors:

- Minimum of 3
- Qualifications:
    - An individual
    - No residency requirement
    - No membership requirement
- Term: 1-year default, five year maximum
- Quorum: Majority
- Committee: 1 director minimum

Officers:

- A president, secretary, treasurer and other officers as appointed by the board. One officer prepares minutes for the directors' and members' meetings and authenticates records.
- The same individual may hold two or more offices.

Members:

- Optional
- Required annual meeting
- Quorum: 1/10th Votes

IOWA

Directors:

- Minimum 1
- Qualifications:
  - An individual
  - No residency requirement
  - No membership requirement
- Term: 1 year
- Quorum: Majority
- Committee: 2 Director minimum

Officers:

- A president, secretary, treasurer and other officers appointed by the board. One officer prepares minutes for the directors' and members' meetings and authenticates records.
- The same individual may hold two or more offices.

Members:

- Optional
- Required annual meeting
- Quorum: 1/10th Votes

KANSAS

Directors:

- Minimum of 1
- Qualifications:
    - A natural person
    - No residency requirement
    - No membership requirement
- Term: Until a successor is elected and qualified
- Quorum: Majority
- Committee: 1 Director minimum

Officers:

- As defined in the board resolution or bylaws. One officer prepares minutes for the directors' and members' meetings and keeps a record.
- The same individual can hold two or more offices.

Members:

- An annual meeting is required if members are entitled to vote for directors.
- Quorum: A majority of those present with proper notice, except in the election of the governing body.

KENTUCKY

Directors:

- Minimum of 3
- Qualifications: None
- Term: 1 year and until a successor is elected and qualified
- Quorum: Majority
- Committee: 2 Director minimum

Officers:

- As defined in the board resolution or bylaws. One officer prepares minutes for the directors' and members' meetings.
- The same individual may hold two or more offices.

Members:

- Optional
- Required annual meeting
- Quorum: 1/10th Votes

LOUISIANA

Directors:

- Minimum of 3. If less than 3, the minimum number of directors needs to be equal to the minimum number of members.
- Qualifications:
    - Natural person
    - No residency requirement
    - No membership requirement
- Term: 1-year default, five year maximum
- Quorum: Majority
- Committee: 2 Director minimum

Officers:

- A president, secretary, and treasurer. Optional one or more vice presidents.
- The officer cannot be a director.
- The treasurer can be a corporation.
- The same individual can hold two or more offices, but they can only sign instruments in one capacity if two signatures are required.

Members:

- Nonstock nonprofit corporations have assumed membership. If there are no members, then the directors become members.
- Required annual meeting.
- Quorum: Majority

MAINE

Directors:

- Minimum of 3
- Qualifications: None
- Term: 1 year
- Quorum: Majority

- Committee: 2 Directors minimum on an executive committee, no minimum for other committees.

Officers:

- A president, secretary or clerk, treasurer and other officers and/or assistant officers as necessary.
- Term: 1 year
- The same individual may hold two or more offices.

Members:

- Optional
- Required annual meeting
- Quorum: 1/10th Votes

MARYLAND

Directors:

- Minimum of 1
- Qualifications: None
- Term: Next annual meeting and until a successor is elected and qualified.
- Quorum: Majority
- Committee: 1 Director minimum

Officers:

- A president, secretary, and treasurer.
- Term: 1 year and until a successor is elected and qualified.
- An individual can hold two or more offices if allowed by bylaws, except the offices of president and vice president. The individual may sign instruments in a single capacity when two signatures are required.

Members:

- If no members exist then, the directors become members.
- Required annual meeting.
- Quorum: A majority of entitled votes.

MASSACHUSETTS

Directors:

- Minimum of 1
- Qualifications:
  - Natural persons
  - No residency requirement
  - No membership requirement

- Term: 1-year minimum, five-year maximum.
- Quorum: Majority
- Committee: 1 Director minimum

Officers:

- A president, treasurer, and a clerk.
- The president must be a director.
- The clerk needs to be a Massachusetts resident unless a resident agent is appointed.

Members:
- If there are no members, then the directors become members.
- Quorum: Majority of entitled votes.

MICHIGAN

Directors:

- Minimum of 3
- Qualifications:
  - May include 1 or more directors aged 16 or 17 years as long as the number isn't half the total of directors required for a quorum to conduct business.
  - No residency requirement

- No membership requirement
- Term: Until next annual meeting and until a successor is elected and qualified.
- Quorum: Majority
- Committee: 1 Director minimum

Officers:

- A president, secretary, and treasurer.
- The same individual may hold two or more offices. The individual may sign instruments in one capacity only if two signatures are required.

Members:

- Optional. Corporations organized as a nonstock can be organized as a membership or directorship basis.
- Required annual meetings unless written consent.
- Quorum: Majority of entitled votes

MINNESOTA

Directors:

- Minimum of 3
- Qualifications:
  - Natural persons

- - The majority must be adults
  - No residency requirement
  - No membership requirement
- Term: 1 year
- Quorum: Majority
- Committee: One or more natural persons, don't need to be directors.

Officers:

- President and treasurer need to be exercised by one or more natural persons.
- The same individual may hold two or more offices. The individual may sign instruments in one capacity only if two signatures are required.

Members:

- Optional. By default, there are no members.
- Required annual meeting.
- Quorum: 1/10th Votes

MISSISSIPPI

Directors:

- No minimum. The number is set by bylaws or articles of incorporation.
- Qualifications:
  - Individuals
  - No residency requirement
  - No membership requirement
- Term: 1-year default, five-year maximum
- Quorum: Majority
- Committee: 2 Directors minimum

Officers:

- As defined by board resolution or bylaws. One officer prepares minutes for the directors' and members' meetings and authenticates records.
- The same individual may hold two or more offices.

Members:

- Optional
- Required annual meeting
- Quorum: 1/10th Votes

MISSOURI

Directors:

- Minimum of 3
- Qualifications:
  - Natural persons
  - No residency requirement
  - No membership requirement
- Term: 1-year default, six year maximum
- Quorum: Majority
- Committee: 2 Directors minimum

Officers:

- A chairman or president or both, a secretary, a treasurer and other officers as appointed by the board. One officer prepares minutes for the directors' and members' meetings and authenticates records.
- The same individual may hold two or more offices.

Members:

- Optional
- Required annual meeting
- Quorum: 1/10th Votes

MONTANA

Directors:

- Minimum of 3
- Qualifications:
  - Individuals
  - No residency requirement
  - No membership requirement
- Term: 1 year
- Quorum: Majority
- Committee: 2 Director minimum

Officers:

- A president, secretary, and treasurer. One officer prepares minutes for the directors' and members' meetings and authenticates records.
- An individual may hold two or more offices.

Members:

- Optional
- Required annual meeting
- Quorum: 1/10th Votes

NEBRASKA

Directors:

- Minimum of 3

- Qualifications:
    - Individuals
    - No residency requirement
    - No membership requirement
- Term: 1 year
- Quorum: Majority
- Committee: 2 Director minimum

Officers:

- A president, secretary, and treasurer. One officer prepares minutes for the directors' and members' meetings and authenticates records.
- The same individual may hold two or more offices.

Members:

- Optional
- Required annual meeting
- Quorum: 1/10th Votes

NEVADA

Directors:

- Minimum of 1
- Qualifications:

- 18 years or older
  - No residency requirement
  - No membership requirement
- Quorum: Majority
- Committee: 1 Director minimum. Non-directors are allowed.

Officers:

- A president or chair, secretary, and treasurer.
- Qualifications: Natural person.
- The same individual may hold two or more offices.

Members:

- Optional
- Required annual meeting unless the election of directors is specified within the bylaws.
- Quorum: 1/10th Votes

NEW HAMPSHIRE

Directors:

- Minimum of 5
- Qualifications:

- ○ At least five voting members can't be from the same family by blood or marriage.
  - ○ No residency requirement
  - ○ No membership requirement
- Quorum: Majority
- Committee: 2 Director minimum

Officers:

- As defined by board resolution or bylaws. One officer prepares minutes for the directors' and members' meetings and authenticates records.
- The same individual may hold two or more offices.

Members:

- Optional. By default, there are no members.
- The only voting rights are those defined in bylaws or articles of incorporation.
- Required annual meeting.
- Quorum: Majority of entitled votes.

NEW JERSEY

Directors:

- Minimum of 3

- Qualifications:
  - 18 years of age or older
  - No citizenship requirement
  - No residency requirement
  - No membership requirement
- Term: 1 year
- Quorum: Majority
- Committee: 1 member minimum

Officers:

- A president, secretary, and treasurer.
- The same individual may hold two or more offices. The individual may sign instruments in one capacity only when two signatures are needed.

Members:

- Optional
- Required annual or biennial meetings
- Quorum: Majority of entitled votes

NEW MEXICO

Directors:

- Minimum of 3

- Qualifications: None
- Term: Until a successor is elected and qualified
- Quorum: Majority
- Committee: 2 Director minimum

Officers:

- As defined by board resolution or bylaws. One officer prepares minutes for the directors' and members' meetings and authenticates records and keeps a record.
- The same individual may hold two or more offices if provided in the bylaws.

Members:

- Optional
- Annual meeting required
- Quorum: 1/10th entitled votes

NEW YORK

Directors:

- Minimum of 3
- Qualifications:
    - 18 years of age or older

- No residency requirement
- No membership requirement
- Term: 1 year
- Quorum: Majority
- Committee: 3 Director minimum

Officers:

- A president, one or more vice presidents, secretary, and treasurer.
- Term: 1 year
- The same individual may hold two or more offices, except for the president and secretary.

Members:

- Optional
- Required annual meeting
- Quorum: Majority of entitled votes

NORTH CAROLINA

Directors:

- Minimum of 1
- Qualifications:
  - Natural person

- No residency requirement
- No membership requirement
- Term: 1 year
- Quorum: Majority
- Committee: 2 member minimum

Officers:

- As defined in the board resolution or bylaws.
- The same individual may hold two or more offices. The individual may sign instruments in one capacity only if two signatures are needed.

Members:

- Optional
- Required annual meeting
- Quorum: 1/10th Votes

NORTH DAKOTA

Directors:

- Minimum of 3
- Qualifications:
  - Individuals
  - No residency requirement

- No membership requirement
- Term: 1-year default, maximum ten years for fixed members
- Quorum: Majority
- Committee: 1 person minimum needs to not be a member or director, except for litigation committees; which need to have a minimum of 1 independent director or another independent person.

Officers:

- A president and secretary
- Qualifications: 18 or older

Members:

- Optional. By default, there are no members.
- Required annual meeting
- Quorum: 1/10th Votes

OHIO

Directors:

- Minimum of 3
- Qualifications: None

- Term: Until a successor is elected
- Quorum: Majority
- Committee: 1 Director minimum

Officers:

- A president, secretary, and treasurer
- Qualifications: Cannot be a director
- The same individual may hold two or more offices.

Members:

- If no members then the directors become members.
- Required annual meeting. The first Monday four months at the close of the fiscal year is the default date.
- Quorum: Voting members presence.

OKLAHOMA

Directors:

- Minimum of 1
- Qualifications:
  - Natural person
  - No residency requirement
  - No membership requirement

- Term: Until a successor is elected and qualified
- Quorum: Majority
- Committee: 1 Director minimum

Officers:

- As defined in the board resolution or bylaws. One officer prepares minutes for directors' and members' meetings and keeps a record.
- The same individual may hold two or more offices.

Members:

- If no members then the directors become members.
- Required annual meeting
- Quorum: 1/3rd members

OREGON

Directors:

- Minimum of 1 for a religious or mutual benefit corporation. Minimum of 3 for a public benefit corporation.
- Qualifications:
  - Individuals
  - No residency requirement

- o   No membership requirement
- Term: 1-year default, five-year maximum
- Quorum: Majority
- Committee: 2 Director minimum

Officers:

- A president and secretary
- The same individual may hold two or more offices

Members:

- Optional
- Required annual meeting
- Quorum: Presence of votes

PENNSYLVANIA

Directors:

- Minimum of 1, default of 3
- Qualifications:
  - o   Natural person of age
  - o   No residency requirement
  - o   No membership requirement
- Term: 1 year
- Quorum: Majority

- Committee: 1 Director minimum

Officers:

- A president, secretary, and treasurer.
- The president and secretary must be a natural person of age.
- The treasurer may be a natural person of age or a corporation.
- The same individual may hold two or more offices.

Members:

- If there are no members, then the directors become members.
- Required annual meeting.
- Quorum: Majority of entitled votes.

RHODE ISLAND

Directions:

- Minimum of 3
- Qualifications: None
- Term: 1-year default, three-year maximum
- Quorum: Majority
- Committee: 2 Directors minimum

Officers:

- A president, secretary, and treasurer.
- Term: 1 year
- The same individual may hold two or more offices except that of president and secretary.

Members:

- Optional
- Required annual meeting
- Quorum: 1/10th Votes

SOUTH CAROLINA

Directors:

- Minimum of 3
- Qualifications:
  - Natural person
  - No residency requirement
  - No membership requirement
- Term: 1-year default, five-year maximum
- Quorum: Majority
- Committee: 2 Directors minimum

Officers:

- A president, secretary, and treasurer.
- The same individual may hold two or more offices.

Members:

- Optional
- Required annual meeting
- Quorum: 1/10th Votes

SOUTH DAKOTA

Directors:

- Minimum of 3
- Qualifications: None
- Term: 1 year
- Quorum: Majority
- Committee: 2 Directors minimum

Officers:

- A president, one or more vice presidents, secretary, and treasurer.
- The same individual may hold two or more offices if provided in the bylaws; except the president and secretary.

Members:

- Optional
- Required annual meeting
- Quorum: 1/10th Votes

TENNESSEE

Directors:

- Minimum of 3
- Qualifications:
    - Natural persons
    - No residency requirement
    - No membership requirement
- Term: 1-year default, five year maximum
- Quorum: Majority
- Committee: 1 natural person minimum who can't be a director

Officers:

- A president and secretary.
- One officer prepares minutes for the directors' and members' meetings and authenticates records.
- The same individual may hold two or more offices, except the president and secretary.

Members:

- Optional
- Required annual meeting
- Quorum: 1/10th Votes

TEXAS

Directors:

- Minimum of 3
- Qualifications: None
- Term: Until a successor is elected, appointed or designated and qualified.
- Quorum: Majority
- Committee: Management committees must have two people and the majority being directors.

Officers:

- A president and secretary.
- The same individual may hold two or more offices, except for president and secretary.

Members:

- Optional
- Required annual meeting

- Quorum: 1/10th Votes

UTAH

Directors:

- Minimum of 3
- Qualifications:
  - Natural person 18 years or older
  - No residency requirement
  - No membership requirement
- Term: 1 year
- Quorum: Majority
- Committee: 2 Director minimum

Officers:

- As defined by board resolution or the bylaws. One officer prepares minutes for the directors' and members' meetings, keeps records and authenticates records.
- Qualifications:
  - Natural person 18 years or older.
  - Doesn't need to be a director.
- The same individual may hold two or more offices.

Members:

- Optional
- Required annual meeting
- Quorum: Presence of voting members

VERMONT

Directors:

- Minimum of 3
- Qualifications:
  - Individuals
  - No residency requirement
  - No membership requirement
- Term: 1-year default, six-year maximum
- Quorum: Majority
- Committee: 2 Director minimum

Officers:

- A president, secretary, and treasurer.
- The same individual may hold two or more offices except for the president and secretary.

Members:

- Optional
- Required annual meeting

- Quorum: 1/10th Votes

VIRGINIA

Directors:

- Minimum of 1
- Qualifications: None
- Term: 1 year
- Quorum: Majority
- Committee: 2 Director minimum

Officers:

- As defined by board resolution or in bylaws. One officer prepares minutes for the directors' and members' meetings and authenticates records.
- The same individual may hold two or more offices.

Members:

- Optional
- Required annual meeting
- Quorum: 1/10th Votes

WASHINGTON

Directors:

- Minimum of 1
- Qualifications: None
- Term: Until a successor is selected and qualified
- Quorum: Majority
- Committee: 2 Director minimum

Officers:

- A president, one or more vice presidents, secretary, and treasurer.
- The same individual may hold two or more offices, except president and secretary.

Members:

- Optional
- Required annual meeting
- Quorum: 1/10th Votes

WEST VIRGINIA

Directors:

- Minimum of 3
- Qualifications: None
- Term: Until a successor is selected and qualified
- Quorum: Majority

- Committee: 2 Director minimum

Officers:

- As defined in the board resolution or bylaws. One officer prepares minutes for the directors' and members' meetings and authenticates records.
- The same individual may hold two or more offices.

Members:

- Optional
- Required annual meeting
- Quorum: Presence of voting members

WISCONSIN

Directors:

- Minimum of 3
- Qualifications:
  - Individual
  - No residency requirement
  - No membership requirement
- Term: 1 year
- Quorum: Majority
- Committee: 3 Director minimum

Officers:

- A president, secretary, and treasurer unless otherwise stated in the bylaws or articles of incorporation.
- The same individual may hold two or more offices.

Members:

- Optional
- Required annual meeting
- Quorum: 1/10th Votes

WYOMING

Directors:

- Minimum of 3
- Qualifications:
    - Individual
    - No residency requirement
    - No membership requirement
- Term: 1-year default, five year maximum
- Quorum: Majority
- Committee: 2 Director minimum

Officers:

- A president, secretary, and treasurer.
- The same individual may hold two or more offices.

Members:

- Optional
- Required annual meetings
- Quorum: 1/10th Votes

APPENDIX -3

LIST OF TAX EXEMPTIONS BY STATE

State	Income Tax Exemption	Sales Tax Exemption
Alabama	Not required Exempt with IRS Determination Letter	Alabama Department of Revenue Form ST: EX-A1 Cost $0
Alaska	Not required Exempt with IRS Determination Letter	Not required No state-level sales tax
Arizona	Not required Exempt with IRS Determination Letter	Arizona Department of Revenue
Arkansas	Arkansas Department of Finance and Administration Form AR1023CT Cost $0	Arkansas Department of Finance and Administration Form F0003
California	California Franchise Tax Board Form 3500 or 3500A	California State Board of Equalization Cost $0

	Cost $25 or $0	
Colorado	Not required Exempt with IRS Determination Letter	Colorado Department of Revenue Form DR 0715 and DR 0716 Cost $0
Connecticut	Connecticut Department of Revenue Services Form REG-1	Not required Exempt with IRS Determination Letter
Delaware	Not required Exempt with IRS Determination Letter	Not required Need to register with Division of Revenue Form CRA
District of Columbia	D.C. Office of Tax and Revenue Cost $0	D.C. Office of Tax and Revenue Cost $0
Florida	Florida Department of Revenue	Florida Department of Revenue Form DR-5 Cost $0
Georgia	Georgia Department of Revenue	Georgia Department of Revenue
Hawaii	Not required Exempt with IRS Determination Letter	Hawaii Department of Taxation Form G-6 Cost $20
Idaho	Not required Exempt with IRS Determination Letter	Idaho State Tax Commission

Illinois	Not required Exempt with IRS Determination Letter	Illinois Department of Revenue Form STAX-1 Cost $0
Indiana	Indiana Department of Revenue Form NP-20A Cost $0	Indiana Department of Revenue Form NP-20 Cost $0
Iowa	Not required Exempt with IRS Determination Letter	Not required
Kansas	Not required Exempt with IRS Determination Letter	Kansas Department of Revenue Cost $0
Kentucky	Not required Exempt with IRS Determination Letter	Kentucky Department of Revenue Form 51A125 Cost $0
Louisiana	Louisiana Department of Revenue	Louisiana Department of Revenue Form R-1048 Cost $0
Maine	Not required Exempt with IRS Determination Letter	Maine Revenue Services
Maryland	Comptroller of Maryland Cost $0	Comptroller of Maryland Form CRA Cost $0
Massachus etts	Massachusetts Department of	Massachusetts Department of Revenue

	Revenue Cost $0	
Michigan	Not required Exempt with IRS Determination Letter	Not required Submit Form 3372
Minnesota	Not required Exempt with IRS Determination Letter	Minnesota Department of Revenue Form ST16 Cost $0
Mississippi	Mississippi Department of Revenue	Not exempt
Missouri	Not required Exempt with IRS Determination Letter	Missouri Department of Revenue Form 1746 Cost $0
Montana	Montana Department of Revenue Cost $0	Not required No state level sales tax
Nebraska	Not required Exempt with IRS Determination Letter	Nebraska Department of Revenue Form 4 Cost $0
Nevada	Nevada Department of Taxation Cost $0	Nevada Department of Taxation Form APP-02.01 Cost $0
New Hampshire	Not required Exempt with IRS Determination	Not required No state-level sales tax

	Letter	
New Jersey	Not required Exempt with IRS Determination Letter	New Jersey Department of the Treasury - Division of Taxation Form REG-1E Cost $0
New Mexico	Not required Exempt with IRS Determination Letter	Not required Exempt with IRS Determination Letter
New York	New York State Department of Taxation and Finance Form CT-247 Cost $0	New York State Department of Taxation and Finance Form ST-119.2 Cost $0
North Carolina	North Carolina Department of Revenue Cost $0	Not Exempt
North Dakota	Not required Exempt with IRS Determination Letter	Not Exempt
Ohio	Not required Exempt with IRS Determination Letter	Not required Exempt with IRS Determination Letter
Oklahoma	Not required Exempt with IRS Determination Letter	Oklahoma Tax Commission Form 13-16-A Cost $0
Oregon	Not required Exempt with IRS	Not required No state-level sales tax

	Determination Letter	
Pennsylvania	Not required Exempt with IRS Determination Letter	Pennsylvania Department of Revenue Form REV-72 Cost $0
Rhode Island	Not required Exempt with IRS Determination Letter	Rhode Island Department of Revenue - Division of Taxation Form EXO-APP Cost $25
South Carolina	Not required Exempt with IRS Determination Letter	South Carolina Department of Revenue Form ST-387 Cost $0
South Dakota	Not required No state or corporate income tax	South Dakota Department of Revenue Cost $0
Tennessee	Not required Exempt with IRS Determination Letter	Tennessee Department of Revenue Form RV-F1306901 Cost $0
Texas	Texas Comptroller Form AP-204, AP-205, AP-206, AP-207 or AP-209 Cost $0	Texas Comptroller Form AP-205-2 Cost $0
Utah	Utah State Tax Commission Form TC-161 Cost $0	Utah State Tax Commission Form TC-160 Cost $0

Vermont	Not required Exempt with IRS Determination Letter	Not required Exempt with IRS Determination Letter
Virginia	Not required Exempt with IRS Determination Letter	Virginia Department of Taxation Form NP-1 Cost $0
Washington	Washington Department of Revenue	Washington Department of Revenue
West Virginia	West Virginia State Tax Department	West Virginia State Tax Department Form F0003 Cost $0
Wisconsin	Not required Exempt with IRS Determination Letter	Wisconsin Department of Revenue Form S-103 Cost $0
Wyoming	Not required No corporate income tax	Wyoming Department of Revenue

CPSIA information can be obtained
at www.ICGtesting.com
Printed in the USA
BVHW032206101222
653950BV00029B/868